LOCH NESS MONSTER
SIMPLIFIED

LOCH NESS MONSTER SIMPLIFIED

SOLOMON HATHAWAY

Revitalized Occult and Strange

Loch Ness Monster Simplified
Author: Solomon Hathaway
Publisher: Revitalized Occult and Strange, an imprint of
Bald and Bonkers Network LLC
Genre: Non-Fiction, Myths and Legends

ISBN/SKU: 979-8-3302-5764-5
EISBN: 979-8-3302-5765-2

Published by Revitalized Occult and Strange, an imprint
of Bald and Bonkers Network LLC.

CONTENTS

CHAPTER 1

Introduction

The Loch Ness Monster, also known by its Scottish Gaelic name Uilebheist Loch Nis and affectionately called Nessie, is an iconic figure in Scottish folklore purported to dwell in the depths of Loch Ness in the Scottish Highlands. Often described as massive in size with a long neck and one or more humps protruding from the water, Nessie has captured the public's imagination since achieving worldwide notoriety in 1933. The evidence supporting its existence is largely anecdotal, consisting of various controversial photographs and sonar readings.

The scientific community typically regards Nessie sightings as a combination of hoaxes, imaginative thinking, or incorrect identification of mundane objects. Cryptozoology, a field labeled as pseudoscience by mainstream researchers, has persistently pursued evidence of Nessie's existence.

Name Origin

In August 1933, the Courier reported George Spicer's claimed encounter with an unidentified creature, sparking widespread fascination. Numerous accounts followed, describing sightings of a "monster fish," "sea serpent," or "dragon," which culminated in the term "Loch Ness Monster." From the 1940s onward, this enigmatic being has been endearingly referred to as "Nessie," a name derived from Scottish Gaelic: Niseag.

CHAPTER 2

Sightings of the Creature

People can find the latest reported sightings of the Loch Ness Monster by visiting: https://www.lochness-sightings.com/

Saint Columba (565)

The first recorded account of a creature in the vicinity of Loch Ness is found in the 7th-century AD work "Life of St. Columba" by Adomnán. In this text, Saint Columba, an Irish monk, encounters the Picts burying a man near the River Ness, who they claim was attacked and pulled underwater by a "water beast" during a swim. Columba then instructs his follower, Luigne moccu Min, to cross the river. As the creature emerges, Columba's invocation of the cross causes the beast to retreat, an event perceived as miraculous by both Columba's followers and the Picts.

This narrative, occurring in the River Ness and not Loch Ness, is often referenced by proponents as early proof of the creature's existence, dating back to the 6th century. Conversely, skeptics view such tales of water beasts as typical of medieval saintly legends, suggesting Adomnán's account may be a traditional story adapted to a local setting. They argue the tale is distinct from the contemporary Loch Ness Monster mythos, later conflated by enthusiasts. Ronald Binns acknowledges this account as a significant early sighting, yet regards other sightings before 1933 as questionable. Christopher Cairney differentiates Adomnán's account from the current myth by examining historical and cultural contexts, noting the influence of earlier Celtic lore regarding aquatic creatures.

D. Mackenzie (1871 or 1872)

In October of 1871 or 1872, D. Mackenzie from Balnain observed an object in Loch Ness that appeared to be a log or an overturned boat, which was "wriggling and churning up the water." The object then accelerated and moved away rapidly. This sighting was not disclosed publicly until 1934, when Mackenzie recounted the event in a letter to Rupert Gould, coinciding with the heightened public interest in the Loch Ness Monster.

Alexander Macdonald (1888)

In 1888, Alexander Macdonald, a mason from Abriachan, reported observing "a large stubby-legged animal" emerging from Loch Ness and approaching within 50 yards of the shore where he was positioned. He conveyed his account to Alex Campbell, the Loch Ness water bailiff, characterizing the creature as similar in appearance to a salamander.

Aldie Mackay (1933)

On May 2, 1933, The Inverness Courier

published a seminal article about a mysterious entity in Loch Ness. The piece, penned by Alex Campbell, a water bailiff and occasional journalist, detailed Aldie Mackay's account of witnessing a massive creature, reminiscent of a whale, undulating through the waters. This sighting occurred as she and her spouse journeyed along the A82 on April 15, 1933. It is believed that Campbell's report was the first to label the entity as a "monster," though there are claims that the term was actually introduced by the editor, Evan Barron. The narrative not only captured the creature's dynamic presence and the disturbance it caused in the loch but also acknowledged the pre-existing local lore of a "beast" residing in the depths, a tale that Mackay conceded to be familiar with. The 1933 article by Campbell also alluded to the longstanding mythos surrounding Loch Ness as the abode of a formidable creature.

George Spicer (1933)

The modern fascination with the Loch Ness Monster was reignited by an encounter on July 22, 1933, when George Spicer and his wife witnessed an unusual creature crossing the road in front of their vehicle. They reported seeing a creature with a substantial body, a long undulating neck, and no visible limbs, which moved swiftly towards the loch, disturbing the underbrush in its path. Spicer compared the creature to a prehistoric animal or a dragon, noting it appeared to be carrying "an animal" in its mouth. The Courier's report of this incident on August 4, 1933, captured the public's imagination, leading to an influx of purported sightings and cementing the term "Loch Ness Monster." Subsequent analysis by researchers posited that Spicer's description may have been influenced by the depiction of a dinosaur-like beast in the then-popular movie King Kong, suggesting the possibility that the account was embellished.

Hugh Gray (1933)

On November 12, 1933, Hugh Gray captured what is believed to be the first photograph of the Loch Ness Monster near Foyers. The image was slightly blurred, and some observers noted that the head of a dog was visible. Gray had been walking his Labrador that day, leading to speculation that the photo actually shows his dog retrieving a stick from the loch. Others suggested it might depict an otter or a swan. The original negative was lost, but in 1963, Maurice Burton acquired two lantern slides made from the original negative. When projected, these slides revealed what appeared to be an otter rolling at the surface.

Arthur Grant (1934)

In the early hours of January 5, 1934, motorcyclist Arthur Grant claimed to have nearly collided with the creature near Abriachan, at the northeastern end of the loch. Grant, a veterinary student, described the creature as having a small head attached to a long neck, resembling a cross between a seal and a plesiosaur. He sketched the creature, and zoologist Maurice Burton suggested it matched the appearance and behavior of an otter. The poor lighting conditions may have contributed to Grant's exaggerated perception of the creature's size. Paleontologist Darren Naish later suggested Grant might have seen an otter or a seal and subsequently embellished his account.

"Surgeon's Photograph" (1934)

The "surgeon's photograph," reportedly the first image of the monster's head and neck, was allegedly taken by London gynecologist Robert Kenneth Wilson and published in the Daily Mail on April 21, 1934. Wilson claimed to have seen the monster and snapped four photos, but only two were clear. The first photo, which became famous, shows a small head and back, while the second, blurrier photo shows a similar head in a diving position. The photo was considered evidence of the monster's existence for decades, though skeptics suggested it depicted driftwood, an elephant, an otter, or a bird. Analysis in 1993 suggested the object in the photo was small, about 2 to 3 feet long.

In 1994, the photo was revealed to be an elaborate hoax. Christian Spurling, the son-in-law of Marmaduke Wetherell, admitted in 1991 that the "monster" was a toy submarine with a head and neck made from wood putty. The hoax was reportedly perpetrated by Wetherell, Spurling, Ian Wetherell, and Maurice Chambers in retaliation for the Daily Mail ridiculing Wetherell over false Nessie footprints.

Taylor Film (1938)

On May 29, 1938, South African tourist G. E. Taylor filmed something in Loch Ness for three minutes on 16mm color film. The film, obtained by science writer Maurice Burton, was not shown to other researchers. Burton published a single frame in his 1961 book, concluding it was a floating object rather than an animal.

William Fraser (1938)

On August 15, 1938, William Fraser, chief constable of Inverness-shire, wrote a letter asserting the monster's existence and expressing concern about a hunting party equipped with a custom-made harpoon gun intending to capture the creature. He doubted his ability to protect the monster from these hunters. The letter was released by the National Archives of Scotland in 2010.

Sonar Readings (1954)

In December 1954, sonar readings from the fishing boat Rival III detected a large object following the vessel at a depth of 146 meters (479 feet) for 800 meters (2,600 feet) before contact was lost. Previous sonar attempts had been inconclusive or negative.

Peter MacNab (1955)

On July 29, 1955, Peter MacNab took a photograph at Urquhart Castle showing two long black humps in the water. The photo was not made public until it appeared in Constance Whyte's 1957 book. In 1958, the Weekly Scotsman published the photo, which some researchers considered a wave effect from three closely traveling trawlers. Others believed it to be a hoax, noting discrepancies between the original negative and the published photo, suggesting it had been doctored.

Dinsdale Film (1960)

On April 23, 1960, aeronautical engineer Tim Dinsdale filmed what he believed to be a dark hump creating a wake as it crossed Loch Ness. Dinsdale, who was on his last day of searching, described the object as mahogany red with a blotch on its side when seen through binoculars. He captured 40 feet of film as the object moved. A 1966 JARIC report analyzing the film suggested the object was "probably animate." Despite further efforts and claimed sightings, Dinsdale could not provide additional photographic evidence.

In 1993, Discovery Communications enhanced the Dinsdale film for a documentary, revealing a shadow in the negative not visible in the developed film. The enhancement seemed to show the rear body of a creature underwater, leading the analyst to reconsider their skepticism about the Loch Ness Monster. However, subsequent analyses suggested Dinsdale likely filmed a boat in poor lighting conditions. JARIC's estimates of the object's size and speed were found to be overestimates due to camera angle miscalculations and film cuts. Critics argue the dark shape seen in the Discovery documentary was probably shore reflections rather than a creature's body.

Most researchers do not consider Dinsdale a hoaxer but criticize his susceptibility to confirmation bias and reliance on dubious sources.

"Loch Ness Muppet" (1977)

On May 21, 1977, Anthony "Doc" Shiels, camping near Urquhart Castle, took what he claimed were some of the clearest pictures of the Loch Ness Monster. Shiels, a magician, said he summoned the creature and described it as an "elephant squid," with the long neck being its "trunk" and a white spot as its eye. The absence of ripples led many to declare the photos a hoax, earning the name "Loch Ness Muppet" for their staged appearance.

Holmes Video (2007)

On May 26, 2007, Gordon Holmes, a laboratory technician, recorded a video of what he described as a "jet black thing, about 14 meters (46 feet) long, moving fairly fast in the water." Loch Ness watchers considered it among the best footage ever seen. BBC Scotland and STV News North Tonight broadcast the video. Marine biologist Adrian

Shine suggested the footage might show an otter, seal, or water bird.

Sonar Image (2011)

On August 24, 2011, boat captain Marcus Atkinson photographed a sonar image of a 1.5-meter-wide (4.9 feet) unidentified object following his boat for two minutes at a depth of 23 meters (75 feet). Atkinson ruled out the possibility of a small fish or seal. In April 2012, a scientist from the National Oceanography Centre identified the image as a bloom of algae and zooplankton.

George Edwards Photograph (2011)

On August 3, 2012, skipper George Edwards claimed that a photo he took on November 2, 2011, showed "Nessie." Edwards, who had searched for the monster for 26 years and spent 60 hours per week on the loch, compared the creature's appearance to a manatee but not a mammal. Other researchers questioned the photo's authenticity, suggesting it might show a fiberglass hump used in a National Geographic Channel documentary.

Inconsistencies in Edwards' claims about the photo's location and conditions led to further skepticism. Although Edwards admitted in October 2013 that his 2011 photograph was a hoax, he maintained that a 1986 photograph was genuine.

David Elder Video (2013)

On August 27, 2013, tourist David Elder presented a five-minute video of a "mysterious wave" in Loch Ness, caused by a 4.5-meter (15 feet) "solid black object" just below the surface. Elder captured the movement while photographing a swan. Sceptics suggested the wave might have been caused by a gust of wind.

Apple Maps Photograph (2014)

On April 19, 2014, it was reported that a satellite image on Apple Maps showed a large creature, possibly the Loch Ness Monster, just below the surface of Loch Ness. The image, taken at the loch's far north, appeared to show a 30-meter (98 feet) long object. Possible explanations included the wake of a boat, seal-caused ripples, or floating wood.

Dakota Frandsen (2018)

During a holiday from Idaho, USA, Dakota Frandsen reported seeing a large dark shape, roughly 40 feet long, near the Urquhart Castle jetty between 3:00 and 3:30 pm. The shape seemed to avoid boat traffic but surfaced briefly when a black speedboat passed by. Frandsen described the object's skin as gray, similar to a hippopotamus, before it swam towards the shore opposite the castle and disappeared. Other similar shapes appeared briefly and vanished quickly.

Drone Footage (2021)

In September 2021, a live-stream near Loch Ness reportedly captured a 20-foot (6.1 meters) creature.

CHAPTER 3

Searches for the Creature

Edward Mountain Expedition (1934)

After reading Rupert Gould's book, *The Loch Ness Monster and Others*, Edward Mountain funded a search of Loch Ness. Starting on July 13, 1934, twenty men equipped with binoculars and cameras monitored the loch from 9 am to 6 pm for five weeks. Although they took 21 photographs, none provided conclusive evidence. On September 15, 1934, supervisor James Fraser filmed the loch, but the footage has since been lost. Zoologists and natural history professors who reviewed the film concluded it likely showed a seal, possibly a grey seal.

Loch Ness Phenomena Investigation Bureau (1962–1972)

The Loch Ness Phenomena Investigation Bureau (LNPIB) was established in the UK in 1962 by Norman Collins, R.S.R. Fitter, politician David James, Peter Scott, and Constance Whyte to study Loch Ness and identify the creature known as the Loch Ness Monster or determine the causes of the reports. In 1967, World Book Encyclopedia granted $20,000 to fund a two-year program of daylight watches from May to October. The principal equipment included 35 mm movie cameras on mobile units with 20-inch lenses and one with a 36-inch lens at Achnahannet, near the midpoint of the loch. The mobile units covered about 80% of the loch's surface. Later, the society's name was shortened to the Loch Ness Investigation Bureau (LNIB), which disbanded in 1972. The LNIB, funded by annual subscription fees, mainly encouraged groups of self-funded volunteers to watch the loch from vantage points with film cameras and telescopic lenses. From 1965 to 1972, it had a caravan camp and viewing platform at Achnahannet and sent observers to various locations around the loch. According to the bureau's

1969 annual report, it had 1,030 members, with 588 from the UK.

Sonar Study (1967–1968)

D. Gordon Tucker, chair of the Department of Electronic and Electrical Engineering at the University of Birmingham, volunteered his services as a sonar developer and expert at Loch Ness in 1968. This was part of a larger effort led by the LNPIB from 1967 to 1968, involving collaboration between volunteers and professionals in various fields. Tucker chose Loch Ness as the test site for a prototype sonar transducer with a maximum range of 800 meters (2,600 feet). The device was fixed underwater at Temple Pier in Urquhart Bay and directed at the opposite shore, creating an acoustic "net" through which no moving object could pass undetected. During the two-week trial in August, multiple targets were identified. One target was likely a shoal of fish, but others moved in ways not typical of shoals, at speeds up to 10 knots.

Robert Rines Studies (1972, 1975, 2001, 2008)

In 1972, a team of researchers led by Robert H. Rines from the Academy of Applied Science conducted an extensive search for the Loch Ness Monster. Using a Raytheon DE-725C sonar unit anchored at 11 meters depth, they detected a moving target estimated to be 6 to 9 meters in length. Specialists from Raytheon, Simrad (now Kongsberg Maritime), and MIT analyzed the data, suggesting the presence of a 3-meter protuberance, potentially from two animals swimming together. Concurrently, an underwater camera with a floodlight captured a pair of photographs showing what appeared to be a rhomboid flipper. Sceptics later dismissed these images as depicting the Loch's bottom, air bubbles, or natural formations.

In 1975, Rines conducted a second search, yielding photographs of unknown animals under murky conditions. One photo seemed to show a plesiosaur-like head, neck, and torso, while another resembled a horned gargoyle head. Critics argued these were likely logs or natural formations, akin to a tree stump later observed during Operation Deepscan in 1987.

In 2001, the Academy videotaped a V-shaped wake and an object resembling a carcass on the loch floor, alongside marine clamshells and unusual fungus-like organisms. These findings suggested a potential connection to the sea.

By 2008, Rines theorized the creature might be extinct, citing declining sonar readings and eyewitness accounts. His final expedition aimed to locate a carcass, exploring the impact of climate change on the creature's habitat.

Operation Deepscan (1987)

Operation Deepscan, conducted in 1987, involved 24 boats equipped with echo sounding equipment scanning across Loch Ness. Initial sonar readings suggested unidentified objects of significant size and strength. Further analysis indicated debris on the loch bottom, with some images showing motion, possibly seals entering the loch. Sonar expert Darrell Lowrance noted anomalies in the data, hinting at potentially new species or un-explained phenomena.

Searching for the Loch Ness Monster (2003)

In 2003, the BBC funded an expedition to Loch Ness employing 600 sonar beams and satellite tracking. Despite high-resolution capabilities that could identify small objects like buoys, no large animals were discovered. Scientists involved, despite their initial hopes, acknowledged that this provided evidence against the existence of the Loch Ness Monster. The expedition was featured on BBC One.

Adrian Shine and Kongsberg Maritime (2016)

Adrian Shine from The Loch Ness Project and VisitScotland collaborated with Kongsberg Maritime to conduct a survey of Loch Ness using an underwater robot. During their exploration of the lake's depths, they located the remains of a prop used in Billy Wilder's 1970 film "The Private Life of Sherlock Holmes." Designed by Wally Veevers, the prop initially featured a neck and two humps, which were later removed at Wilder's request. This alteration affected its buoyancy, causing it to sink during a filming test.

DNA Survey (2018)

In June 2018, an international team from the universities of Otago, Copenhagen, Hull, and the Highlands and Islands conducted a DNA survey of Loch Ness to investigate the presence of unusual species. Published in 2019, their results indicated the absence of DNA from large fish such as sharks, sturgeons, and catfish, as well as from otters or seals. However, the survey detected a significant amount of eel DNA, suggesting a large population of small eels rather than one or more large individuals. Professor Neil Gemmell of the University of Otago, who led the study, noted that while they found no evidence of giant eels, the possibility of exceptionally large specimens could not be ruled out. He also stated that no reptilian DNA sequences were found, leading to the conclusion that a large scaly reptile is unlikely to inhabit Loch Ness.

High-Tech 2023 90th Anniversary Search

In August 2023, a high-tech search took place over a weekend to commemorate the 90th anniversary of the 1933 Aldie Mackay sighting. Organized by Loch Ness Exploration volunteers in collaboration with the Loch Ness Visitor Centre, the search utilized advanced technologies including sonar for mapping the lakebed, thermal imaging drones for surface scans, and hydrophones (underwater microphones) which captured some recorded sounds, speculated to be from ducks. Despite significant participation and live-streamed coverage attracting hundreds of viewers, no conclusive sightings were reported.

CHAPTER 4

Possible Explanations

Various explanations have been proposed to explain sightings of the Loch Ness Monster. According to Ronald Binns, a former member of the Loch Ness Phenomena Investigation Bureau, there is likely no single explanation for the creature. Binns, who authored skeptical books such as "The Loch Ness Mystery Solved" in 1983 and "The Loch Ness Mystery Reloaded" in 2017, argues that human psychology plays a significant role in these sightings, where the eye sees what it expects to see. He categorizes sightings as misidentifications of known animals, inanimate objects or effects, reinterpretations of Scottish folklore, hoaxes, and the possibility of exotic species of large animals. A reviewer described Binns as evolving into the definitive skeptic on the subject, emphasizing that he does not dismiss sightings as hoaxes but views them as a sociological phenomenon, a myth in the true sense of the term. Binns suggests that interest in the possibility of the monster's existence persists among a small group who prioritize eyewitness accounts above other evidence.

MISIDENTIFICATION OF KNOWN ANIMALS

Eels: Early theories suggested a large European eel as a possible explanation for the Loch Ness Monster due to their presence in the Loch. However, sightings were dismissed by Tim Dinsdale due to eels' side-to-side undulating motion, unlike the reported serpentine movements.

In recent years, a comprehensive DNA study conducted from 2018 to 2019 confirmed the presence of European eels in Loch Ness. This research found no DNA evidence supporting the existence of large animals such as catfish, Greenland sharks, or plesiosaurs. Many scientists now hypothesize that giant eels could account for many, if not most, of the reported sightings.

Elephant: In 1979, biologist Dennis Power and geographer Donald Johnson suggested that the famous "surgeon's photograph" depicted the head, trunk, and flared nostrils of a swimming elephant, possibly photographed elsewhere and falsely attributed to Loch Ness. Palaeontologist Neil Clark later proposed that elephants from travelling circuses might have bathed in the loch, with their trunks and backs mistaken for the monster's humps and neck.

Greenland Shark: Zoologist Jeremy Wade investigated the Loch Ness Monster in 2013 for the series "River Monsters" and theorized it could be a Greenland shark. These sharks, known to reach lengths of up to 20 feet, inhabit the North Atlantic and are dark in color with a small dorsal fin. Biologist Bruce Wright suggested that Greenland sharks could potentially survive in freshwater, using rivers and lakes to find food, including Loch Ness's abundant salmon and other fish.

Wels Catfish: In 2015, Steve Feltham proposed that the monster might be an unusually large Wels catfish, possibly released into the loch during the late 19th century. This theory gained attention after Feltham's vigil at the loch, recognized by the Guinness Book of Records.

Other Resident Animals: Binns and others have noted that judging the size of objects in water, especially through telescopes or binoculars without external references, can lead to misinterpretations. Loch Ness is home to resident otters and has documented photos of deer swimming in the loch, which could contribute to misidentified sightings. Birds flying low over the water have also been mistaken for the "head and neck" of a creature.

MISIDENTIFICATIONS OF NON-LIVING OBJECTS OR NATURAL PHENOMENA:

Boat Wakes: Reports of wakes have surfaced even when Loch Ness is calm and devoid of nearby boats. Bartender David Munro reported observing what he believed to be a creature zigzagging, diving, and resurfacing, with 26 other witnesses from a nearby car park allegedly corroborating his sighting. While some accounts describe V-shaped wakes resembling those caused by boats, others describe shapes inconsistent with typical boat wakes.

Trees: In 1933, the Daily Mirror published a photograph with the caption suggesting that a peculiarly shaped tree trunk washed ashore at Foyers on Loch Ness might explain reported monster sightings.

Tree Logs: In a series of 1982 articles for New Scientist, Maurice Burton suggested that sightings of Nessie and similar creatures might be attributed to Scots pine logs that ferment and rise to the surface of the loch. These logs, initially sealed by resin, could eventually release gases due to decomposition, propelling them through the water with their branch stumps resembling descriptions of the monster.

Seiches and Wakes: Loch Ness, owing to its elongated shape, experiences unusual ripples on its surface. Seiches, large oscillations caused when water returns to its natural level after being displaced to one end of the lake, create standing waves. Loch Ness has a seiche period of approximately 31.5 minutes. Although seismic activity in Scotland is typically too mild to generate observable seiches, major earthquakes elsewhere can produce significant waves. Historical records note severe seiches in Loch Ness following events like the 1755 Lisbon earthquake, although no monster sightings coincided with these occurrences.

Optical Effects: Wind conditions can create a choppy appearance on the water's surface, while calm patches may appear dark, reflecting the surrounding mountains and clouds. Atmospheric refraction can distort the appearance of objects and animals, as demonstrated by W. H. Lehn in 1979 with a photograph of a mirage resembling a head and neck on Lake Winnipeg.

Seismic Gas: Italian geologist Luigi Piccardi has proposed geological explanations for ancient myths and legends, suggesting that seismic activity along the Great Glen Fault could release gas through the fault, creating disturbances on the water's surface that might be mistaken for submerged creatures.

FOLKLORE

In 1980, Swedish naturalist and author Bengt Sjögren noted that contemporary beliefs in lake monsters such as the Loch Ness Monster have roots in kelpie legends. According to Sjögren, accounts of lake monsters have evolved over time; originally portraying horse-like creatures, these tales were designed to deter children from approaching the loch. Sjögren observed that kelpie legends have transformed into descriptions reflecting a modern understanding influenced by plesiosaurs.

The notion of the kelpie as a water horse in Loch Ness was referenced in a Scottish newspaper in 1879, which inspired Tim Dinsdale's Project Water Horse. Research into pre-1933 Highland folklore reveals frequent mentions of kelpies, water horses, and water bulls, with Loch Ness being the most commonly cited location.

HOAXES

Numerous attempts to perpetrate hoaxes surrounding the Loch Ness Monster have occurred, some successfully deceiving the public. Other hoaxes were quickly exposed either by their creators or through diligent investigation. Several notable examples include:

- In August 1933, Italian journalist Francesco Gasparini published what he claimed to be the first news article on the Loch Ness Monster. In 1959, he reported seeing a "strange fish" and fabricated eyewitness accounts to elevate the creature to the status of a monster.

- In the 1930s, big-game hunter Marmaduke Wetherell claimed to have found footprints of the monster, which turned out to be tracks from a hippopotamus-foot umbrella stand.

- In 1972, a team of zoologists from Yorkshire's Flamingo Park Zoo discovered a large body floating in the water, which was later revealed to be a disfigured bull elephant seal planted in the loch as a prank.

- On July 2, 2003, Gerald McSorely claimed to have discovered a fossil from the Loch Ness Monster, which upon examination was found to have been planted.

- In 2004, a Five TV documentary team used special effects to create an animatronic model of a plesiosaur named "Lucy," attempting to convince viewers of its existence in the loch.

- In 2005, two students publicized a large tooth found embedded in a deer on the loch shore, which was later revealed to be a muntjac antler used as a publicity stunt for a horror novel.

EXOTIC LARGE ANIMAL

Plesiosaur: In 1933, speculation arose suggesting that the Loch Ness Monster resembled the extinct plesiosaur, a long-necked aquatic reptile that disappeared during the Cretaceous–Paleogene extinction event. However, this theory has faced several rebuttals:

- Leslie Noè from the Sedgwick Museum in Cambridge, in an October 2006 article in New Scientist titled "Why the Loch Ness Monster is no plesiosaur," asserted that the anatomy of the plesiosaur's neck precludes it from lifting its head out of the water in a swan-like manner.
- The Loch Ness itself is relatively young, forming around 10,000 years ago at the end of the last ice age after being frozen for approximately 20,000 years.
- If creatures resembling plesiosaurs inhabited Loch Ness, they would need to surface frequently to breathe, making regular sightings more likely.

In response to these criticisms, proponents like Tim Dinsdale, Peter Scott, and Roy Mackal proposed the idea of a marine creature possibly descended from or resembling a plesiosaur due to convergent evolution. Robert Rines suggested that certain sightings' "horns" could function as breathing tubes, allowing the creature to breathe without fully surfacing. Recent findings have indicated that plesiosaurs had some ability to inhabit freshwater, though the cold temperatures of Loch Ness would present challenges for their survival.

Long-necked Giant Amphibian: R. T. Gould posited the concept of a long-necked newt, while Roy Mackal explored this possibility and assigned it a high probability (88%) on his list of potential candidates.

Invertebrate: In 1968, F. W. Holiday proposed that Nessie and other lake monsters, such as Morag, might be large invertebrates like bristle-worms, citing the extinct Tullimonstrum as a comparable example due to its shape. Holiday argued that this theory could explain sightings on land and the variable appearance of the creature's back, likening it to medieval descriptions of dragons as "worms." However, Mackal found this theory less convincing compared to eels, amphibians, or plesiosaurs.

CHAPTER 5

References

- Krystek, Lee. "The Surgeon's Hoax". unmuseum.org. UNMuseum. Archived from the original on 8 May 2019. Retrieved 21 April 2015.
- Life of St. Columba Archived 17 August 2016 at the Wayback Machine (chapter 28).
- Mac Farlane, Malcolm (1912). *Am Faclair Beag*. Stirling: Eneas MacKay, Bookseller. Archived from the original on 3 August 2020. Retrieved 17 January 2020.
- Carroll, Robert Todd (2011) [2003]. *The Skeptic's Dictionary: A Collection of Strange Beliefs, Amusing Deceptions, and Dangerous*

Delusions. John Wiley & Sons, Inc. pp. 200–201. ISBN 978-0-471-27242-7. Archived from the original on 16 October 2021. Retrieved 15 November 2020.

- Binns, R. *The Loch Ness Mystery Solved*. pp 19–27.
- Daily Mirror, 11 August 1933. "Loch Ness, which is becoming famous as the supposed abode of a dragon..."
- The Oxford English Dictionary. 9 June 1933 as the first usage of the exact phrase Loch Ness monster.
- Campbell, Elizabeth Montgomery & David Solomon. *The Search for Morag*. Tom Stacey, 1972. ISBN 0-85468-093-4, page 28 gives an-t-Seileag, an-Niseag, a-Mhorag for the monsters of Lochs Shiel, Ness, and Morag, adding that they are feminine diminutives.
- "Up Again". *Edinburgh Scotsman*. 14 May 1945. p. 1. So "Nessie" is at her tricks again. After a long, she has by all accounts bobbed up in home waters...
- Carruth, J. A. *Loch Ness and its Monster*. Abbey Press, 1950. Cited by Tim Dinsdale (1961) *Loch Ness Monster*, pp. 33–35.

- Adomnán. p. 176 (II:27).
- Binns, R. *The Loch Ness Mystery Solved*. pp. 52–57.
- Binns, R. *The Loch Ness Mystery Solved*. pp. 11–12.
- Bro, Lisa; O'Leary-Davidson, Crystal; Gareis, Mary Ann (2018). *Monsters of Film, Fiction and Fable, the Cultural Links Between the Human and Inhuman*. Cambridge Scholars Publishing. pp. 377–399. ISBN 9781527510890.
- Mackal, Roy. *The Monsters of Loch Ness*.
- *The Mammoth Encyclopedia of the Unsolved*.
- Bignell, Paul (14 April 2013). "Monster mania on Nessie's anniversary". *The Independent*. Archived from the original on 11 December 2019. Retrieved 18 January 2020.
- Searle, Maddy (3 February 2017). "Adrian Shine on making sense of the Loch Ness monster legend". *The Scotsman*. Archived from the original on 15 February 2020. Retrieved 18 January 2020.
- Williams, Gareth (2015). *A Monstrous Commotion: The Mysteries of Loch Ness*. Orion Publishing Group. p. 105. ISBN

978-1-4091-5875-2. Archived from the original on 5 August 2020. Retrieved 18 January 2020.

- Gould, Rupert T. (1934). *The Loch Ness Monster and Others*. London: Geoffrey Bles.
- Delrio, Martin (2002). *The Loch Ness Monster*. Rosen Publishing Group. p. 48. ISBN 0-8239-3564-7.
- "Loch Ness Monster: Is Nessie just a tourist conspiracy?". *BBC News*. 12 April 2013. Retrieved 25 January 2024.
- *Inverness Courier*. 2 May 1933. "Loch Ness has for generations been credited with being the home of a fearsome-looking monster".
- Campbell, Steuart (14 April 2013). "Say goodbye to Loch Ness mystery". *The Scotsman*. Archived from the original on 11 December 2019. Retrieved 18 January 2020.
- "Report of strange spectacle on Loch Ness in 1933 leaves unanswered question – what was it?". *The Inverness Courier*. 11 September 2017. Archived from the original on 21 February 2020.
- Hoare, Philip (2 May 2013). "Has the internet killed the Loch Ness monster?". *The*

Guardian. Archived from the original on 12 December 2019. Retrieved 18 January 2020.

- "Is this the Loch Ness Monster?". *Inverness Courier*. 4 August 1933.
- Dinsdale, T. (1961). *Loch Ness Monster*. p. 42.
- "Are Hunters Closing in on the Loch Ness Monster?". *The Scotsman*. Retrieved 15 March 2022.
- "Did King Kong inspire Nessie?". *The New Zealand Herald*. 17 August 2014. Retrieved 20 July 2023.
- Edwards, Phil (21 April 2015). "How scientists debunked the Loch Ness Monster". *Vox*. Retrieved 13 August 2023.
- Mackal, R. (1976). *The Monsters of Loch Ness*. p. 85.
- Loxton, Daniel; Prothero, Donald. (2015). *Abominable Science! Origins of the Yeti, Nessie, and Other Famous Cryptids*. Columbia University Press. pp. 142–144. ISBN 978-0-231-15321-8.
- Burton, Maurice. "A Ring of bright water?" *New Scientist*. 24 June 1982. p. 872.
- Campbell, Steuart. (1997). *The Loch Ness*

Monster: The Evidence. Prometheus Books. p. 33. ISBN 978-1573921787.

- Dinsdale, T. *Loch Ness Monster*. pp. 44–45.
- Burton, Maurice. "A Fast Moving, Agile Beastie." *New Scientist*. 1 July 1982. p. 41.
- Burton, Maurice. (1961). "Loch Ness Monster: A Burst Bubble?" *The Illustrated London News*. May, 27. p. 896.
- Naish, Darren. (2016). "Hunting Monsters: Cryptozoology and the Reality Behind the Myths". *Arcturus*.
- Mackal, R. P. (1976). *The Monsters of Loch Ness*. p. 208.
- "The Loch Ness Monster and the Surgeon's Photo". *Museumofhoaxes.com*. Archived from the original on 6 August 2014. Retrieved 28 May 2009.
- "A Fresh Look at Nessie". *New Scientist*. v. 83, pp. 358–359.
- Chapman, Douglas. *Nessie – The Surgeon's Photograph – Exposed*. Archived 14 January 2012 at the Wayback Machine.
- Martin, David S. & Alastair Boyd (1999). *Nessie – the Surgeon's Photograph Exposed*.

East Barnet: Martin and Boyd. ISBN 0-9535708-0-0.

- "Loch Ness-odjuret – Historien bakom bilden » Moderskeppet".
- "Loch Ness Hoax Photo". *The UnMuseum*. Archived from the original on 8 May 2019. Retrieved 28 May 2009.
- "Nessie's Secret Revealed". *yowieocalypse.com*. Archived from the original on 4 January 2015. Retrieved 3 January 2015.
- Harmsworth, Tony. "Loch Ness Monster Surface Photographs. Pictures of Nessie taken by Monster Hunters and Loch Ness Researchers". *loch-ness.com*. Archived from the original on 13 February 2015. Retrieved 3 January 2015.
- *The Loch Ness Story*, revised edition, Penguin Books, 1975, pp. 44–45.
- *Ness Information Service Newsletter*, 1991 issue.
- Burton, Maurice. (1961). *The Elusive Monster: An Analysis of the Evidence From Loch Ness*. Hart-Davis. pp. 83–84.
- Casciato, Paul (28 April 2010). "Loch Ness Monster is real, says policeman". *Reuters*.

Archived from the original on 2 June 2016. Retrieved 28 April 2010.

- "Police chief William Fraser demanded protection for Loch Ness Monster". *Perth Now.* 27 April 2010. Archived from the original on 28 October 2021. Retrieved 7 February 2012.
- "Searching for Nessie". *Sansilke.freeserve.co.uk*. Archived from the original on 31 May 2009. Retrieved 28 May 2009.
- Binns, Ronald. (1983). *The Loch Ness Mystery Solved*. Prometheus Books. p. 102.
- Campbell, Steuart. (1991). *The Loch Ness Monster: The Evidence*. Aberdeen University Press. pp. 43–44.
- "The MacNab Photograph" Archived 19 April 2017 at the Wayback Machine. The Museum of Hoaxes.
- "The Loch Ness Story", revised edition, Penguin Books, 1975, pp. 64–65.
- Gilder, E.R. (1967). *The Rines Search: The Hunt for the Loch Ness Monster*. London: Geoffrey Bles.
- "Loch Ness Is Just Another Animal Mystery,

Scientist Declares". *San Francisco Examiner*. 12 March 1968.

- Binns, R. (1984). *The Loch Ness Mystery Solved*. pp. 105–106.
- "The Mystery of the Loch Ness Monster". *Scientific American*. February 1975. pp. 89–93.
- Binns, R. (1983). *The Loch Ness Mystery Solved*. Prometheus Books. pp. 89–90.
- "Loch Ness Monster". *Encyclopaedia Britannica*.
- "The Loch Ness Monster". *Natural History Museum*. 18 August 2014. Retrieved 2 April 2019.
- The Loch Ness Monster: The Evidence, by Steuart Campbell. W.W. Norton & Company, 1986.